This book belongs to:

_____

Preface

Let's face it. Driving on our roads is becoming more dangerous as the number of accidents happening is increasing every year. A part of the problem is that people are driving recklessly and are too distracted by their cell phones. Another factor is that many people do not pay attention to road signs and some persons are not aware of what they mean. This book was created with the intention of helping to address the latter. It aims to give you information on more than 40 different traffic signs that people don't normally know as well as inform you as to what they mean and how you should react upon seeing them.

Additionally, you will also be given other such information as to what the color used on a traffic sign says about it. At the end of reading this book, you will be given a multiple-choice quiz to help you to practice what you have learned. Feel free to share this book with your friends and family and help make our roads safer.

What does a road sign color say about it?

Red

The color Red is used for road signs that alert you to stop or yield. Red is used for stop signs, yield signs, do not enter signs, and wrong way signs.

Green

The color Green is used for road signs that give direction. It is used on signs that tell you the name of the street, exit signs, mile markers, and signs giving you directions and distance to a specific place.

Blue

The color Blue is usually used on signs that display information on services for travelers. These signs inform motorists where they can find rest areas, tourist sites, hospitals, hotels, gas stations, restaurants, campgrounds, picnic areas, and other places visited by travellers.

Yellow

The color Yellow is used on road signs that warn of potential hazards or changing road conditions. Some signs that use yellow include narrow bridge ahead signs, unpaved road surface signs, a hidden cross street and curve ahead road signs.

Orange

The color Orange is used on road signs that are usually related to road work, temporary traffic control, and maintenance. If you see an orange road sign, be on the lookout for workers.

Curve Ahead

This sign alerts you to an upcoming curve along the roadway . It also informs you that the route you are traveling has more than one curves, bends or corners.

Crosswind Danger

This sign alerts you to the danger of crosswind in the area that you are traveling. Upon seeing this, you should slow your speed to minimize the risk of accident.

Narrow Bridge

This sign alerts you to the fact that the bridge that you are about to cross is narrow. Extra precaution should be taken as you traverse the bridge.

Steep Descent

This sign alerts you to the fact that you are about to travel down a steep hill. Care should be taken by slowing your speed so as to maintain control of your vehicle.

Loose Gravel

This sign alerts you to the danger of loose gravel along the roadway. You should slow down as your vehicle may spin out of control. Loose gravel can also cause damage to your vehicle and others.

Narrowing Ahead

This sign alerts you to the fact that the road will become more narrow ahead.

Unpaved Roadway

This sign alerts you to the fact that you are about to travel along an unpaved section of road. You should slow your speed as the ride will become bumpy.

Right then Left Turn

This sign alerts you to the fact that you are about to make a right turn followed by a left turn. You should slow your speed in anticipation of this.

Left then Right Turn

This sign alerts you to the fact that you are about to make a left turn followed by a right turn. You should therefore drive in anticipation of this and slow your speed.

Two Way Traffic

This sign informs you of the fact that you are about to enter a zone where there is traffic travelling in two directions.

Maximum Height

This sign alerts you to the fact that you are about to travel in an area where there is limited height. In this case the maximum height is 3.5 meters.

Pass Left or Right

This sign alerts you of an obstacle in the road ahead. It directs you to pass left or right of the obstacle.

Uncontrolled Crossroad

This sign informs you of the fact that there is an uncontrolled crossroad up ahead. It informs you that the road is crossing from the right.

Emergency Vehicles

This sign alerts you to the fact that you are about to travel in an area where emergency vehicle frequent so you should be on the lookout for them.

Stop and Give Way

This sign informs you that you are to stop and give way to oncoming traffic ahead of you.

Falling Rocks Risk

This sign informs you of the fact that there is a possibility of rocks falling along the route of travel. You should take extra precautions when travelling here.

Side Road Merging

This sign alerts you to the fact that there is a side road merging onto the main that you are traveling. You therefor should be on the lookout for other cars as they may be in a blind spot.

Roadworks Ahead

This sign informs you that you are about to travel within an area where there is road works taking place. You should be on the lookout for worker along the roadway.

Playground Warning

This sign informs you of the fact that there is a playground in the area that you are travelling. You should therefore be on the lookout for kids playing.

Roundabout Ahead

This sign informs you of the fact that you are about to travel around a roundabout.

Slippery Road Surface

This sign informs you that you are about to travel within an area where the roadway is slippery especially when it is wet. Upon seeing this you should slow down.

Narrowing on both Sides

This sign informs you of the fact that the roadway you are traversing narrows on both side. You therefore need to pay keen attention while driving.

Truck Rollover Warning

This sign informs you of the fact that you are travelling around curves where trucks traveling at excessive speeds have a potential to rollover.

Low Ground Railroad

This sign alerts drivers of long wheelbase vehicles or trailers of a potential hang-up situation at the crossing. Therefore extra care should be taken by these drivers.

Right Curve Intersection

This sign informs you of the fact that the roadway you are traversing will intersect with another lane or road on the right curve ahead of you. You therefore be on the lookout as you make the corner.

Intersection Ahead

This sign alerts you to the fact that you are about to approach and intersection. You should slow your speed in anticipation of this.

Flagger Ahead

This sign alerts drivers to the fact that a flagger is controlling traffic ahead. You should therefore be on the lookout for them so you can follow their directions.

Rough Road Ahead

This sign informs you of the fact that the roadway you are traversing will get rough or bumpy ahead. You should therefore slow your speed or be in anticipation of a bumpy ride.

Uneven Road Surface

This sign alerts you to the fact that the road surface will get uneven as you continue driving ahead. You should slow your speed in anticipation of this.

Right Lane Ends Ahead

This sign alerts drivers to the fact that the right lane that they are travelling along will end ahead of them. They should therefore, be prepared to merge into the left lane.

Merging Lane

This sign informs you of the fact that you are traversing along a roadway which will converge with another lane ahead. You should be prepared and be on the lookout for the drivers that will merge into your lane.

Sharp Turn Reduce Speed

This sign alerts you to the fact that a sharp turn is coming up ahead of you. It also advices you that should reduce your speed in anticipation of this.

Yield Ahead

This sign informs you of the fact that merging drivers must prepare to stop if necessary and allow drivers on another approach to proceed.

Railway Without Barriers

This sign informs you of the fact that there is a Railway Crossing Without Barriers ahead of you. You should therefore take extra precaution.

U-Turn Ahead

This sign informs you of the fact that you are about to make a U-Turn. You therefore should slow your speed and be prepared to do so.

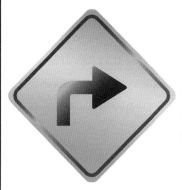

Sharp Right Turn

This sign informs you that you are about to make a sharp right turn ahead of you. You should prepare by slowing your speed.

Sharp Left Turn

This sign informs you that you are about to make a sharp left turn ahead of you. You should prepare by slowing your speed.

No Right Turns

This sign informs you of the fact that right turns are prohibited. Therefore you should not make any right turns until another sign advices you otherwise.

No Left Turns

This sign informs you of the fact that left turns are prohibited. Therefore you should not make any left turns until another sign advices you otherwise.

No U-Turns Allowed

This sign informs you of the fact that U-turns are prohibited. Therefore you should not make any U-Turns until another sign advices you otherwise.

No Straight Ahead

This sign informs you of the fact that straight-through driving is prohibited at the junction that you have come to, and also that you are required to turn either left or right.

No Heavy Goods Vehicles

This sign informs you of the fact that vehicles carrying heavy goods, such as trucks, are prohibited from driving on the road that it is posted.

Multiple Choice Quiz

1. What warning does this sign give?

A. There is a U-Turn coming up.
B. The right lane ends ahead of you.
C. The road surface is uneven.
D. There is a sharp right turn coming up.

2. What information does this sign give?

A. The road you are traveling on is slippery.
B. The road you are traveling is about to get bumpy.
C. There is a risk of falling rocks on this road.
D. No small cars are allowed on this road.

3. What does this sign tell you to do?

A. Stop and give way to oncoming traffic ahead
B. Pass left or right of the obstacle.
C. Turn right at the intersection.
D. Stop and continue forward.

4. What color is used on signs that warn of potential hazards or changing road conditions?

A. Red
B. Yellow
C. Orange
D. Green

5. What color is used is usually used on signs that display information on services for travelers?

A. Red
B. Yellow
C. Blue
D. Green

6. You are about to drive on a section of roadway that is unpaved. Which of the following signs will alert you of this?

A.

B.

C.

D.

7. You are about to drive on a section of roadway that is slippery especially when it gets wet? Which of the following signs will alert you of this?

A.

B.

C.

D.

8. You are about to drive across a bridge that is narrow. Which of the following signs inform you of this?

A.

B.

C.

D.

9. You are traveling along a roadway that has a high risk of loose gravel. What sign should be posted to inform you of this?

A.

B.

C.

D.

10. The color red is used on signs that:

A. alert you to stop or yield.

B. give direction.

C. display information on services for travelers.

D. are related to road work and maintenance.

11. The color Orange is used on signs that:

A. alert you to stop or yield.

B. give direction.

C. display information on services for travelers.

D. are related to road work and maintenance.

12. What does this sign warn you about?

A. Loose gravel.

B. Slippery road surfaces.

C. Crosswinds.

D. Steep hill.

13. What does this sign warn you about?

A. Low ground railway.

B. Slippery road surfaces.

C. Uneven road surfaces.

D. Steep hill.

14. You are traveling along a roadway on which you cannot make a U-Turn? Which sign would be posted to inform you of this?

A.

B.

C.

D.

15. You have come to a junction where straight-through driving is prohibited. Which sign would be posted to inform you of this?

A.

B.

C.

D.

16. You are traveling along a section of roadway where heavy goods vehicles are not allowed. What sign will be posted?

A.

B.

C.

D.

Answer Key

1.
B. The right lane ends ahead of you.

2.
C. There is a risk of falling rocks on this road.

3
A. Stop and give way to oncoming traffic ahead

4
B. Yellow

5.
C. Blue

6.
D

7.
D

8.
B

9.
A

10.
A. alert you to stop or yield.

11.
D. are related to road work and maintenance.

12.
C. Crosswinds.

13.
A. Low ground railway.

14.
C..

15.
D..

16.
C..

Notes:

Notes:

Printed in Great Britain
by Amazon

18849606R00016